John
MacKenzie

SLEDGEHAMMER

and other
poems

Polestar Book Publishers
Vancouver

Polestar Book Publishers and Raincoast Books acknowledge the ongoing support of The Canada Council; the British Columbia Ministry of Small Business, Tourism and Culture through the BC Arts Council; and the Government of Canada through the Book Publishing Industry Development Program (BPIDP).

Design by Val Speidel
Author photo by Christine Trainor
Printed and bound in Canada

Credits:
"Hearthouse," "As Strands of Sun," "Our Divergence Was First A Delta," and part of "Far From the Sea" were originally published in *blue SHIFT: a journal of poetry*. "On the sixth day I was pissed & . . ." was first published in *The Buzz*. A version of "Lamentations at Gravity's Feet" was published as part of *blue SHIFT*'s "john eats the little book" limited-edition chapbook series.

CANADIAN CATALOGUING IN PUBLICATION DATA

MacKenzie, John, 1966-
   Sledgehammer and other poems

   ISBN 1-896095-56-9
   Title
PS8575.K425S53 2000   C811'.54   C99-911337-2
PR9199.3.M327S53 2000

Library of Congress Catalogue Number: 99-069297

Polestar Book Publishers,
an imprint of Raincoast Books
8680 Cambie Street
Vancouver, British Columbia
Canada
V6P 6M9

5 4 3 2 1

for Connor

(in case he ever needs it)

and for the record

Contents

Acknowledgements / 7

fragrant as metal *(from the west)*

Me as an Archaeologist / 11

Our Divergence Was First a Delta / 13

As Strands of Sun / 14

A List (By Colour) of Things Left Behind / 15

on hands and darkness / 16

Box O' Glass / 18

Someday I Will Give You Back Your Love / 19

hearthouse / 20

Just These Few Roses (On the Day Divorce Takes Effect) / 22

Lamentations at Gravity's Feet / 24

coda: the moon in pieces (like a heart) / 41

pocket of sky *(through the centre)*

on the sixth day I was pissed & . . . / 45

Far from the Sea (Portage la Prairie, MB) / 47

Seeing Ontario from a Greyhound / 52

Riding the Route for Nature and Health / 53

Note to my few friends (with rant attached) / 56

Because I speak too rarely / 58

Lower the Boom / 59

sledgehammer *(to the east)*

Sledgehammer / 65

Landscape, from lowdown / 66

Meditation on the Memory of the Landscape of a Perfect Self / 68

When the Discussion Became an Argument Loud as Time / 71

Drinking with the Neurosurgeon / 73

Why the Elephant of Elephant Rock Got Up and Walked Away / 75

Do Not Write Love Poems Near the Sea / 77

The Surface [:] Viscosity of Want / 79

This Binary Perception / 80

He Kept to Himself, Mostly / 81

My love is strung with the ancient / 83

Where I First Saw the Light / 85

In Lieu of Flowers / 87

Mouths Hunger / 90

The Integrity of Life and Death / 91

The Farmer Thinks About Cows and Fish / 93

The Whole Shebang / 95

Momentary Silver (Between Sackville and the Sea) / 97

the machinery of my tongue, this scent of a flower / 99

O We Burnt Out Our Clutches (Riding Them Buggies of Need) / 100

The Idea of Beauty (Spoke Itself) / 101

tanka / 102

Acknowledgements

Although I write poetry as consistently and unavoidably as a body sweats to maintain temperature, this book would never have existed without the support and encouragement of many people. So a few thank-you's are in order: to Catherine Matthews, for showing me that to continue is possible; to John Cox and Christine Trainor, for pointing out that I sometimes write with a sledgehammer; to my editor Lynn Henry, for knowing when a poem is finished – and, more importantly, when a poem isn't finished; to Chris Molyneaux, for filling tables with food (and clearing pool tables); to the owners, staff, and regulars at Cedar's Eatery and Baba's Lounge, for time, space, and criticism; and to Marty Field, for reminding me about music.

fragrant as metal

(f r o m   t h e   w e s t)

Your love, your body

the knife that cut me

open to my bliss.

—CHRISTOPHER DEWDNEY

Me as an Archaeologist

I dig into your city; piece together your shattered pottery of desire.
I find bone fragments & tea leaves.
Bronze arrowheads of lust. Petrified, unleavened love.
Your fossil eyes gleam with salt.

In a dusty corner, I find flax seeds; plant flax.
Watch it sprout green as your youth, blossom
blue as your hot Mediterranean sea;
turn it into crisp linen.

I turn back crisp linen & sleep every night
between cool dreams of olives embroidered with spun gold.

Ancient gods sing. Their voices are streams of white
galaxies.
Below us the earth sings in a voice of dark loam & granite.

The moon, a rough & worn coin, wishes us luck in our madness,
our night of being wolves in the grey mountains.

I brush dirt, chip sediment from the hearth where you kept time,
where time hung in beaten copper kettles
full of lentils, barley & bay leaf, maybe parsley.

Your larder is full of old rice & desiccated pine nuts.

I dig into the rubble of your city & find
all these things preserved.
I know where your house is; I touch the old stone walls.

I want to hang a beaten copper kettle over your hearth,
fill it with brown rice, pine nuts,
strips of spring lamb. Season it all with cinnamon.

I want goat cheese, unleavened bread, wine ...
the strong wine of your youth
when grapes grew & grew under the lucky silver moon.

I want to mix your strong wine with water,
drink from your pieced-together desire.

Our Divergence Was First a Delta

Our divergence was first a delta forested with questions
where doubt perched, feathered, hook-beaked, sank its talons
into new species of hope.

Today a continent lies between us. This new ocean is quiet,
goose-pimpled by cool rain. My flesh, too, tightens into bumps
at this wide kiss; remembers

another shore where your mouth, wet, tidal,
brought me close before our hair, full of sand, carried
the taste of salt inland

As Strands of Sun

It is clear my life is a slow drift, slow
as strands of sun through darkness,
to collisions   eruptions of heat.

Held together by static charges,
I could dissipate
every moment   (dandelion seeds).

Flown from east to west, I seek
solace in stones, dark earth
stronger than orchids   fragrant as metal.

A List (By Colour) of Things Left Behind

A singular perception of green

White gusts of laughter, like this wind
Full of petals

A string of perfect, round moments
Ground to powder

One pair of boots, black and scuffed;
The rundown clocks of their heels

One blue sky, slightly used

Too many words (also down-at-the-heel)
From faces down at the mouth

My son's eyes
(But not his first, slow blink)

on hands and darkness

I don't know her. But
as partial payment for reading my palm, I give her —
hammered into a medallion purple as a bruise — ten years of my life.
Smiling, she puts them in her jeans.

She is from Alberta. Her forehead hints of broad plains.
Her hair ripples in the wind she rolls on her tongue.
She likes the salt in it, says it enhances the taste of home.
She drinks more water.

"Light is perilous," she tells me.
"So, for you, I've turned what I see into sounds that will echo in darkness."

"Are you left-handed?" she asks in the middle of the reading.
"Not quite," I say, thinking of lost pool games.
You see, she's had to search my other hand for fragments of belief,
broken bits of desire.
And the child line confuses her. Faint, she tells me,
distant blue, like hills losing oxygen ... something about the perspective.

When she asks my relation to Escher, I think of my son in another country,
The one bigger than us that we've swallowed,
that swallows us —
I think her shrug means movement would help.

She speaks of darkness and sacred descents. (Now I'm confused.)
"Try one," she says. "They're small."
As the sun crosses my left shoulder and my hands fall into shadow,
I start to follow; then look up, expecting her to be gone.
But no, it's not like that. She's no ghost —
At least, not one of mine.

I see her later that night,
blurred hands spinning three leather-wrapped sticks in the air.
"To erode the palms," she explains,
like my lost decade worn against her thigh.

The last thing she tells me is that stars —
like sparks smouldering into a quilt —
exist only to burn the night that would be perfect without them …
a hand with no lines, frictionless.

Box O' Glass

I want to crush the stars, she said
and stepped into the sky
Stepped into the sky
as you or I would step
into our homes

She didn't stand in the sky like some ancient goddess
She was older than that
older than the sky
(maybe she made the big night
that made the sky)

She picked a casual handful of stars
braided a rope of light
and tied it to the moon
She made the moon a flail
and smashed the stars

Galaxies were heaps of broken glass
she swept into a box
The moon fell in
What a lovely sound, she said,
and danced

Someday I Will Give You Back Your Love

The Moon fell into my stomach
And I was full of want.
My hands were empty of everything I touched.
The sky shredded itself when I looked up.
My eyes were mouths.

The Moon dropped through my stomach
And I was empty from the knees up.
I ate the world with a glance,
I chewed planets. I was unsatisfied
(Someday I will give you back your love)

My thighs were hollow and prone to folding.
I stood at the center of the galaxy
And screamed. Sparks fell from my lips
And smouldered. Worlds burned.
I was unsatisfied
(Though my mouth was full of words I'd once said)

I hooked one knee over the rim of the Universe
And splashed my foot in Nothingness.
Earth rattled in an empty thigh
Until I placed it in one eye. It melted
And was several glistening tears. My mouth was still full.

hearthouse

for my son, Connor

the heart holds its own heat,
the heart is its own furnace,
its own fuel

you are the house of my heart
from your tiny limbs   to the lengthening
curl of your red-tinged hair   to your eyes
(just like my eyes) when I come home to them
in my mind

(I come home to a pile of gravel
we scraped together, a pile of gravel and
a rough piece of wood for a chimney)

my heart burns & pumps
heat through you & you
reciprocate   your reciprocal

heat floods through me with the clank & thud of old
radiators in the house of my
heart love is the familiar

creak & sigh of expanding pipes as water
changes temperature & circulates
as you circulate

in my veins & the arteries of my mind   you are central
heating the house of my heart

Just These Few Roses
(On the Day Divorce Takes Effect)

& where do you go from all this burning green spotted with
                    remnants of roses?
survivors of wind & punching rain aerating this
patch of unkempt beauty
this chaotic strew of rosebushes &
long-leafed grasses
untrimmed trees & mysterious thickets diked by red slabs of sandstone
walked dogs & shiny wind-suited tourists   their sleek manmade
clothes gleaming
like money
like the glazed eyes of chemists & molecular engineers building gore-tex
& dacron universes
searching for molecules to depend futures from

& the sun sinks through all this
through you (& the greying curious beard paused beyond your left
shoulder &
the fat blond baby raising a fist in salute from his assembly-line stroller)

the sinking sun builds an evening wind
from the different cooling rates of water & air
& the wind blows cold through photons creeping towards you
slower than a strobe-light

& you figure & figure   calculate powers of ten   try to
find the volume of need by measuring the length & width of want
the height of indifference

but it's August & you are left with these few crinkled roses
& the vague scent of what they were

Lamentations at Gravity's Feet

We are all falling. This hand's falling too —
all have this falling-sickness none withstands.
— RAINER MARIA RILKE

... I am wondering about the colour green.
Why it hurts like sound hurts inside a jar ...
— ANNE CARSON

When I met you, the moon was full
It has waned and waxed many times since we parted

Like some ancient Arab poet, I feel sand in my teeth
When I remember you and fires in the night

This city is a desert scattered with forgotten stones
Arranged in blackened rings

We talked over the beat of hooves in the night
And meant to ride the trail of stars

This crescent moon is the hook
On which I've hung myself to wait

December, and snowflakes hang
Like ropes from gallows

Where has the wind gone
That would blow the stink off this?

Under this snow are roots
Sheathed like knives in the ground

Wait, wait, wait

Here at gravity's feet,
Even time crawls

Is there time yet beneath twisted boughs?
The sun has gone down again

When the pond blackens,
The span of thumb and forefinger supports the world

The swing of the axe is a circle
The creak of the ice is a crack in the sky

Cold feet, brittle boots
Euclid whispers at the perimeter

At least, with snow,
Where you have been, disappears

Your lips were softer than any I'd kissed
And the cards said love lay ahead

Amid candles and silk and the aftertaste of tea
I learned about chocolate

Sometimes, when the moon was a fist in your stomach,
You lay over my knees, head on my chest

I can still see the curl of your fists
As you squeeze the moon into dust

Disembodied, I miss your weight;
Alone, I taste you in tea

Five years ago today
Our son was conceived

We forgot about the candles
Until I wondered at your smokiness

My mouth on you, my mouth on you

The bedding under the shower, you under me
Under you, earth under heaven

You surprised me
By asking for him

The trees in this light —
Sharp as knives

The butcher, an angel, says,
"Flesh is best kept frozen."

Once I came home to taste dirt;
After the meal, my tongue rusted

This is the colour of saliva:
An iron-orange dust

What is held too long, withers;
Press it in books

We were married in a rattle of leaves
Thrown like dice by the wind

As a prayer
I tied green round my waist

I still haven't learned to kneel
Except before flowers

I've plucked an infinity of petals —
All the multiples of minus one

I am uprooted, toppled
By relentless green

Each morning one spring, I ground barley into feed
Fattened cattle for others while we thinned

We lived in watercolours —
The sun a smear in the washed-out sky

Fade to black

Where were you as I lay between galaxies,
While vacuum pulled harsh skies through me?

I've rolled every star on my tongue, spat
Streams of nebulae through my teeth

And I've fallen to earth ... one more stone angel
Broken in gravity's hand

Down here I've looked in every brook for the colour of your eyes,
Your sound of my name

This is where I live now,
In these spaces where nothing coheres

Above places even crows have abandoned, dragonflies dance
On wings they've woven from sackcloth and hope

I am weary
And my skin has become grey

Ashes … a rain of ashes …
This earth a desert of ash

I have not seen a crow for days —
But this morning the sun rose with a croak

(Imagine green sparks as sunlight hammers
Flight on a sweep of black wings)

[ee equals emcee squared]

The seed, everything peeled away by teeth,
Strains to pass into green

It was the rain piercing my skin
That dried me to this

Chained to the sun, I am pulled
Out of dark soil like a tooth

Light flashes like hail, makes my teeth gongs;
My feet trail a whole light-year behind

The old man with white wild hair insists
The faster I go, the heavier I get

All is flux, and contingent upon observation
(Your shadow engraved on every wall)

Beneath molecules of duty, atoms of love,
Strange particles crash

A quantum need, too small to observe, is inferred
From the behaviour of larger things

Like water over stones, glass over centuries,
Desire moves under its own weight

Wisteria, convolvulus, honeysuckle, morning glory dance
As we did: left around right … *do si do*

At the foot of the ladder what matters is perspective:
The distance between each rung doubles

I'd wrestle an angel if I could find one ...
Where are you hiding, Michael, wings folded?

I hear the thunder of your climb
Feel your wind like a wall against my face

One white feather drifts, blood bright on its edges —
From a wing, or a prayer?

I'll wait; lie here with stones as pillows,
Lips pressing the dark thighs of earth

[q times p is not equal to p times q]

We cannot mind both our p's and our q's
When p refers to a particle's momentum and q to its position

You recede, or I was there;
You were here, or I proceed

If a smile both is and isn't, it widens to infinity
Choice is stretched too thin to see

Here time smears as easily as fingerprints, or lipstick
Effect divorces cause

The flowers we never planted are beautiful —
This is why I water stones

The earth is stripped — what soil remains is loose
As flesh over starved bone

Again children faint with hunger in the streets
They fall down to die in the dust

The horn of compassion is broken
Parents test the thighs and biceps of children

The cooking fires are lit … the water drawn
And hung in pots to boil

Once I removed my heart, hoping it would harden
The streets remained dry, the children thin

I am swallowed

Gravity gives as it takes
Presses me against an earth shaken with desire

Even the heavens have been pulled down,
Blanket me in the glory of night

I may kneel here forever, head bowed
As I return and return

The tears of gods fall, sweet rain;
Water turns to wine, flesh becomes bread

(I have borrowed this meal from a prophet
His seasonings were wormwood and gall, bitterness and woe)

Though I turn and turn about,
My way is blocked with salt-whitened stone

Like Jeremiah, I am set
"In dark places like the dead of long ago"

I have cried out in protest and prayer
My voice is the wind in bare trees

I have given all the water of my body in tears;
The grass still yellows and withers

coda: the moon in pieces (like a heart)

Thin, bloodless
a scar on a swollen lip.

An open mouth ready
to speak,
or spit before she closes

on you;
swallows.

Thin? thin as a pull tab, twisted
on the half-open sky

listen! the heavens hiss.

A pale wax seal pressed
on a dark letter; the indecipherable stars

scrawled behind her like
a doctor's scrip.

She hangs
like a drop of hot weld

pocket of sky

(t h r o u g h   t h e   c e n t r e)

What humbles these hills has raised

the arrogance of blood and bone ...

—TED HUGHES

on the sixth day I was pissed & ...

I made them, these
rough, young Rockies raised
recklessly from the earth

— treading heavy-footed, it was my anger
sank the Great Lakes
& sent

wave after wave
of dust-flinging rocks
westward

to pile atop each other,
canted & crooked, some
kicked sideways

& some upside-down,
asses
in the clouds

— I made them, & these
foothills suddenstopped
in awe,

running up
each other's arses in imitation
of these

still predators, whose teeth
rip open
the bellies of clouds,

who spit shreds
& rain;
chew the sky

to this
blue,
soft leather

Far from the Sea (Portage la Prairie, MB)

> *It is impossible to draw lines that delineate*
> *separate categories of air, soil, water and life.*
> — DAVID SUZUKI, The Sacred Balance

The sea is east of us, the sea is west of us,
the sea is many millions of years behind us, but
we feel her rhythms, her tidal dance in capillaries; feel
ghosts of currents rush through
this new green risen from her fossil bed.

... However, this planet
still
spins on its axis

and down here, among grain and cash crops,
I listen to the rush of growth —
and the canola, the screaming yellow rapeseed forces me to worship
strange, blue flax.

This prairie, this flattening manitoba, rolls me out thin —
here on this alien surface, in this exotic landscape,
I stutter through days drowning
in the constant pneumatic yammer of my heart.
I know you ... your heart has bled into me, transfused me.
You are my heart. You carry
granite and salt across this flat land

(once I believed the ancient & sacred ball of your belly could drive
our waltz forever).

This soil holds the thunder of herds, dark secrets.
Bison were an ocean,
and the ocean taunted the moon above it.

The earth is the enemy in this place,
deep black foreign soil clings like velcro: clench fistfuls —
feel it creep under fingernails, lodge against the quick?

On a late jurassic plain the diplodocus died,
decayed, descended — long before the jaded jurassic.
As seas slid through rift valleys and lay panting on the continent
cowturtles and swinelizards fertilized the soil,
became earth.

Now I work a dour Scot's fields (salt of the earth,
sweat of my brow); this earth is his enemy. Like a politician,
he is sworn to plant this same old
ground black with blood that blooms bone-white
in winds that descend like empty stomachs
over these fields
bordered by trees thin as hope ...

But bones are the only sure crop
on this prairie that spreads us out like water, pulls me
into a stutter of waves
as I work harrows in diagonals across quarter-sections
and the rattle and thump behind me
takes the homogenous surface apart.

Black earth churns behind me,
breaks down further with each pass,
turns over and over like thoughts disassembling — the same old soil,
the same old thoughts the harrows pull out of context.

Hard little seeds of prayer lurk among granules,
teeth pull frayed orange snags of baling twine and
a green fluttering hope that all this work will work —
that this ritual rending into straight lines will force
molecules to dialogues with sun and rain — Listen! to the upward
surge of growth ...

If we stop now
all history will drown us in bones and blood
under this top-heavy green.

As it is, the black earth pushes up stones
between seasons. The earth bucks as a rodeo bull,
all stabbing, scissoring horns and dust-kicking hooves driven
by tendons like cables becomes, under the booted rider,
a coil-spring suddenly loosed at both ends.
The black earth cracks and spits herself towards the sky.

And one of these days splinters
of granite and limestone, shards of gold and quartz,
and old bits of iron from drills and combines
and rods from digger chains will fly ...

This earth is black powder under the constant sun
and, as the sea gathers
beyond a fragile isthmus of time,
it hides under a confusion of growth, waves

momentary surrender — bleached flags of wheat and barley
at half-mast above entrenched potatoes and sugar-beets
after a regimental summer of worry and irrigation.

Jesus! Ya cultivate beets at two-and-a-half miles an hour.
The (life preserver) row-crop tires give ya
fuckin highway hypnosis
— don't let 'er veer across the rows!

And the next day a thunderstorm snaps
long whips of hail across all that precision,
and those delicate delicate leaves hang
notched and browning ...
All hail the crop insurance man!

Harvest is a political crisis. A tearing
and shredding of documents. Harvest is
the violent negation of six months' work
when blood runs back, runs black into the soil.

The soil drinks and remembers ...
And in it, the blood roars; as the sea
slapped by the North Wind, awakens
and beats at the blameless shore;
as we, touched by what we won't understand,
drive our anger before us in waves.

There are days when I walk into boulders formed in midair,
when cliffs streaked with sea-salt rear themselves from sidewalks to loom
                between us,
days when all the horses of the world are loosed and the rumble of
                hooves shakes

in my temples,
days when I toss like flotsam,
disappear in your ocean.

There are days when you wash like an early sun across the pale denim of
                my eyes,
when echoes of thighs and the taut muscles of forearms curtail thought,
days when dense pauses inhibit the passage of time,
hasten the passage of us.

Seeing Ontario from a Greyhound (April '95)

because Ontario is overdone in everything
from geographical limits to lawn décor
imagination has merged with the digestive tract

and this mutated system chews deep
into the bones of landscape

the rocks here are shattered moans, birthing
            runty litters of birch

Riding the Route for Nature and Health

Bad things are happening, and that's good.
— MICHAEL LEON

past random apple trees, around hurrying orange caterpillars
between fields of tall corn under a sky refracting
me amid this devastation beyond town
into a roar of front-end loaders, a scrattle of
steel buckets & blades pushing into shale, the crumbling

edges of shale pits lined with garbage, cut
with earthen ramps packed under notched tires of rough dump trucks
& the scarring treads of bulldozers (this one
still toppling trees, ripping earth, tearing out
stumps & roots)

blackberries ripen on the edge of this
red turns to deep purple-blue, stains
my eyes the colour of the bruised sky & rain
falls through the slanted rays of the falling sun while
the wind at my back skirls
like distant bagpipes after my ears, me fleeing

the city building itself out past & over blackberries
filling holes left by extracted trees with concrete & fiberglass
breathing formaldehyde into root systems

& rain falls through
the slanted rays of the falling sun
as I sing

the drone of bike tires on gravel, my sternum buzzing
a deep hum, vibrating trees
drowning machines in sonic waves, the whole
world rattling with my passage &

the sky still is not still, the sky is
still patched with Autumn blues greys & blacks
my laughter rips cloud banks out whole &
throws them down like swatches of Night, pulls
three-mile-wide sheets of Light across the western sky

I turn back to the city, legs pumping
against the solid wall of wind it blows out,
the wind rushing from town bends the flimsy
yellow & orange of butter-and-eggs, the intricate
intermittent white of queen anne's lace, tolls orange
bell-like bunches of dog-berries, makes
whole fields of purple clover rage northward & crash
against treelines like wild alien seas &

my laughter is an array of sledgehammers
slamming fractals in september-tinted air
my howl of dismay the same,
blurring metal cracking through everything torn
everything stolen
everything expropriated

through these still green trees I see
streamlined buses plow dense air between
toppling towers & feel
cool beads of hilarious death in my armpits, a sudden
grinning growth of bone through
the flesh of my jaw.

.

Note to my few friends (with rant attached)

I have stolen your red moon & hung it
In a poem of my own device   To replace it,
I offer this yellow moon as
A curse upon convenience mistaken for progress

For you I have found this yellow moon lowering
Over the city   this yellow moon that is
A screaming saw-blade cutting
Co-axial & fibre-optic cables   this
Yellow moon to topple the CN Tower   the
World Trade Center, world trade

For you this glowing steaming cauldron tipped
Above factories & mines   above the pipes &
Frameworks of refineries   & yes
Above the bulldozers I wanted till one
Ripped the sandstone throat
Out of the brook below home

For you this yellow moon to fill
Holes burnt in the sky (this moon may be
The round mouth of god speaking fish
Back into the oceans & forests of teak back
To bathe in their own sweet rain)

I have found this lowering yellow moon for you
This yellow moon swung like
A wrecking ball over cities   returning
Concrete to dust   steel to oxides &
No particular order
To the placement of flowers

I have found for you this yellow moon I say is
The colour of hope against destruction & despair
This gold coin whose ring
Shatters the countertops & eardrums of bankers & priests

For you this yellow moon to keep
In the pocket of sky

Because I speak too rarely

(By the way, your lips are
what silk aspires to be.)

Sometimes I see your naked shoulders,
the faint pink
traces my stubble leaves.

I see your hackles, the short hairs on the back of your neck
rise
when your head sinks forward.

When your head sinks forward
I could make a charcoal rubbing of your spine,
its slow concave descent
to gently convex muscles & decisive thighs.

Sometimes we are naked in my mind & my mouth searches
in that hollow near your hipbone
or back of one knee.

I see the arrow of your clavicle
Define   your breasts.

Sometimes I taste your salt.
Sometimes my ears are filled with
the soft insistent music of your thighs.

Lower the Boom

for Ivan Arsenault, killed in August 1998
on this framework of steel and rivets,
this erector set pushing into the sky

He stood here before the glass went on, stood
in and on the growing skeleton, grasping
I-beams in the heat of Ontario's August days
palms sweating in leather gloves guiding
I-beams to their appointed places, or else

he tied re-bar with those gloved hands, tied
arcane knots around slender rods
to be hidden in concrete, to hold
the whole damn thing together

This is some of what he did: woke every morning
at 4:30, ate cereal from boxes, drank
tea that steeped while he brushed teeth and shaved,
threw his lunch box in the passenger's seat,
tightened his boot laces and his belt,
mumbled morning talk with the others
in his Miscouche accent while settling
his hardhat on dark hair, thinking maybe

about a daughter starting school soon
maybe about the Jays' game, or
more likely, being from Miscouche, wondering if
the Habs will ever find another goaltender like Dryden or Roy

This is what he did that day: woke at 4:30
ate his cereal, drank his tea
tightened his boot laces and belt and climbed
the naked steel under the climbing sun, all day
he clambered in the ring and clamour
welding this, riveting that, guiding
crane-swung bundles of steel to rest, and

most of the day he breathed
and worked, glowing like a beacon of sweat

and he argued about overtime and cursed bosses (whose wreath —
and the note saying they thought they should send it
— was thrown on the funeral-home lawn)

yeah, he worked and cursed the bosses' bidding
on jobs they couldn't start on time and rushed
to finish on schedule, under budget
he cursed old equipment and mistakes driven by hurry
and the sloppy minds of others, but ...

        the beat of hammers and the view, the
        pure music of storey rising on storey, of
        seeing the metal become

he could hear, some days, the steel breathe
see it pulse and grow like
the child he felt move each morning under
his callused hand on Ruth's belly

He saw the sunset as he thumbed down another bundle
he saw the sunset and, at first, when the steel slammed into him
he thought it was beauty flattening him, he believed
the glorious shattered red and purple had
fallen from the sky into him and
he remembered his Catholic upbringing
and, suddenly, the meaning of epiphany, but

the others saw the scattered red as blood, the paramedics saw
the darkening glorious purple bruise he had become
and the doctor stripped off latex gloves, moved on   Ruth

miscarried

sledgehammer

(t o   t h e   e a s t)

I was born into an ambush

of preachers, propagandists, grafters ...

—MILTON ACORN

Sledgehammer

this is the work of the hammer: to break us open
with its ring & clang in the cracking earth
in the autumn ache of water spread between hills
in all these yellow trees, in the roots of them
in flesh grown dry

in leaves on water
in the black crow you dreamed pecking
in bones & dust
in love made out of bruises & threats of death
in belly-ripping want
in the tears of sex beneath leaning trees
in the white mist

in galleries of trees misted with the breath of gods
(the thick sky like muscles of underslung jaws)
in the awful crack of bones broken at their centres

this is the work of the hammer: to drive everything together
to join & connect hearts to each other
to shape vision & pound & crack & dismantle
to break everything apart
in search of the pure in flesh grown dry
in bones & dust

landscape, from lowdown

I

this Island suffers from a gentility of
low hills that discourage reaching up, for the limits of up
discourage leaping into regions beyond breath
where every contraction of lung has immediate meaning

where a gasp becomes a grasp &
lungs like open hands
become sudden fists in the chest, batter·
through the bony cage of ribs
to be air itself
not collectors, containers, processors

to escape economy-driven reasons for being & how
supply & demand creep into everything, push
our eyes down, keep our hands reaching
down into pockets here
where there are no big rocks to tie ourselves to
— to leap from, if necessary

no, there are no big rocks here, no towering aeons
staring out of time, protruding into present
full of bones so old they've turned to stone
hardened themselves
against dismissal, disappearance

bones waiting for flesh & muscle, tendons
to materialize ... flood with hot blood
& step thunderously out into traffic

thighbones as big as semis to thrust
huge curves of hips against rude rectangular
factories, to grind
this acute age into dust that might
become stone

3 *looking up*

but this Island is the neckbone of some ancient & gentle beast
some immense dragon bathing in the salty gulf, waiting

under the whirling sky, under votive stars
for a moment, for a whim of movement

to coil & wing away dripping red & green
into black, blue
into the white spaces of galaxies

Meditation on a Memory of the Landscape of a Perfect Self

for Catherine

there was a time when the stars were stars
before the focus of my eyes was adjusted
when the stars each had thin and dangerous blades slicing the sky

when I walked under trees
in a scuffle of leaves and the sharp scent of humus
and bones fed themselves, mineral by molecule
to undergrowth

when green was visible math
multiplying everywhere, dividing into shades
and a potato field's mounded rows were laid square
against a headland, green eclipsing red soil

and with every step the green fragmented, shattered into plants
into leaves dancing to the musics of sun and wind
infinite planes of vertical symmetry swaying
at every pulse of my blood

and these eyes, just dissected by stars
were drawn by gravity to one leaf
manufacturing chlorophyll out of earth and water, air and fire

and the stars still slicing forever out of my eyes
whirling their multitudes of two-edged swords
(like the angel guarding the entrance to Eden reflected
                in an eternity of mirrors)
sank beneath furrowed surfaces into a lattice-frame architecture
down to strands of phloem like canals
carrying molecules of carbon to be built into starches and sugars
and emerged through questing root filaments to gaze
across a floating landscape of soil particles

one slim blade of retina slipped into a crack
and was spun from a nitrogen molecule
to pierce a helium atom and lie half-blinded
under a sky fraught with lightning linking protons to electrons
and reflected
gleaming
from the smooth inscrutable faces of neutrons hanging
like freshly minted moons

(and I'm sure I saw left-handed Vulcan
tipping up his visor,
shutting down his arc-welder for the day)

in those days I was awake
at six in the morning eating peanut butter sandwiches
reading the *World Book Encyclopaedia*, dreading
the linear inevitability which elementary school fastens to time
and hearing my future insatiable eyes whispering
that I should miss the bus, start walking

into reservoirs of magic poised in fields and trees
in the hoarseness of crows hopping branch to branch or
prostrating themselves against the immense lip of sky

against the kiss of the goddess who walks
in the texture of skin
in the surface tension of water
whose teeth are this sharp smile

When the Discussion Became an Argument
Loud as Time

Once upon a time there was a man distracted
By his hands — how they grasped
And dug on their own,
How they went wandering intent as scalpels;

How they felt up rocks and leaves,
Broke nails and banged knuckles,
Became blunted and nicked searching
In crevices, in wallets, for love.
And how they kept coming back
To him.

So he thought: Maybe this is the centre —
Maybe this cock, this peg of flesh,
Is what everything spins around,
Depends on, hangs from ...

And so he would grasp it, whiteknuckled,
Till he hung himself from his cock.
Till it was the spear in his side.
And his napalm-leaking wound.

Its uncertain rigidity was the spike that nailed him to each moment
While the hub of time eroded
The small of his back.

Once he looked up from his hands and asked:
Having failed at humanity,
What do I resort to? Religion? Philosophy?
Poetry? — But

His hands took him again, down
Where skin stretched.
And he stared at how his pores gaped,
Rims blackened,
Like uneasy wombs.

Drinking with the Neurosurgeon

So I cut into the head, see
my bone saw squealing and throwing sparks —
it's hard to keep that blade sharp —
smoke drifting in thin blue curls up into the light
me bending and blowing on the pencil lines
to clear the blood and bits of bone enough
to see what the hell I'm doing

I make one cut and then a couple of crosscuts
and the head opens up like a goddamn door, or a window
cut in the wall as an afterthought because
you thought you might want to see
maybe the sunset
maybe the blue herons painted into the cove at dawn
or in this case
what's going on in a guy's head

And the stuff he had jammed in there!
I'd never been that close to a blue heron before
damn thing thought my hand was a mackerel ...
long scissors of a beak came clipping out of the hole —
if one of those sunsets he had stacked beside it hadn't fallen just then
thick with red clouds
and sent that bird flapping back towards dawn
I'd be smoking with my other hand

Yeah, a lot of stuff in there
I'd catch the edge of something with my probe
and a raft of night would go feathering
down towards the brain stem; sometimes studded with nails
sometimes gleaming with bits of dew
and sometimes falling into a bright well at the centre

And below all this, the thing he had lodged
in Broca's Area, all his vocabulary of desire
and commitment arranged round it as spectators
was a four-and-a-half by nine Black Crown pool table
with Simonis cloth — the Pleiades hung over it as lamps
And him and god chalking their cues
smoking cigarettes and playing nineball
"Double, or nothing," he'd say after every game

I closed him up, and as far as I know,
they're still playing

Why the Elephant of Elephant Rock Got Up and Walked Away

Not because the pouring of concrete around her feet
to keep them dry and keep her
under the watchful eye of the Tourism God
was the last straw

not because the constant gawking and oohs and aahs from shore
were wearing her away
quicker than wind and water could

not because a conversion to New Age religiosity
made her reject objectifying by others
as an erosion of her sense of self

not even because rumours of hoaxes involving government
          sculptors driving
backhoes found their way to her ears
over the hiss of chemical sprayers drifting in their own clouds of doubt
down farmers' fields
and over loud water beating rocks into flat earths to be sent skipping
with flicks of wrists into the blue
and even over the crumble of soil and sandstone from the cliffs
          around her
as the Island continued its slow-motion foundering

No, the elephant of Elephant Rock got up and walked away because
she heard a humpback whale groaning with lust
and went to join him
dipping her trunk and splashing salt water ecstatically
over the soft red curves of her back

Do Not Write Love Poems Near the Sea

do not write love poems near the sea

she will hear in the scratch of pens on paper

the rhythms of rocking bodies

the sound of blood rushing to lips

the quick breathy hiss of pupils dilating

and,
especially,

do not write love poems in the sand beside the sea

neither with salt-whitened twigs nor backs

but with knees sincere in composition

and eyes cast down

to see the grains spread their filaments of need

for,
I tell you,

on a night of the new moon

she is an ocean of desire

her kiss deeper than the sky

The Surface [:] Viscosity of Want

Father, he said, O Father ...
Then was silent;
For he had no parent but smoke
And, perhaps, a woman who kept comfort at bay
By opening her arms to all.

In silence, he cherished grief,
Nurtured grief, ate grief,
Shat grief, wore grief as a mask of laughter,
Gave grief like bitter chocolate ...

Dried, withered within the shell of his flesh,
He followed will o' wisps of science, carelessly,
Seeking solidity in details and finding the details
Neither opposed to, nor in favour of solidity —
Dense and separate —
The void in meaning was the meaning in void.

Again he said, Father ...
But the wind only blew, and the grass grew,
And water ran, as it would, through his fingers,
In its own course, deep, under bridges,
Between stones, driving the millwheel of desire.
And all the flowers threw down their petals.

This Binary Perception

So, stuck, caught, jammed between once and soon, next and last,
in this binary perception
time moves on, always, only the now visible
between behind and before ... We can't climb,

jump these walls of either-or, this-that,
and rattle bones of the dead at the unborn, saying,
"Look what has become of you! — this whiteness
gathered in sticks — because yesterday piles up

in heavy, dangerous folds tomorrow reflects ..."

— What is time but an accumulation of darkness
around a seed of light like a pearl,
a poem around a phrase,
an effect around a cause? —

everything because of something — look!
what has become of us
stuck, caught, jammed in either-or because
we believe

we cannot rattle unborn bones at the dead.

He Kept to Himself, Mostly

He was made
like us
of blood and skin
and bits of dust from distant lands
but he could not see into the bone
that built his blood in tiny blocks
He could not see beyond the bone
He could not see into the bone
where hammers fell
and forges flamed
and water cooled and tempered
all the cells
that he was welded from
He did not know that bone marrow
narrow-canalled bone marrow
was the factory of love

And so he walked as we all walk
in a constant controlled fall
and at every shock of thudding foot
the factory
turned out another million cells
and age gathered on him like dust
But he could not see beneath his skin
to the love which built itself
and thundered sonnets
whispered life
and knew that leaves and daisy petals

and oceans
and grinning partial moons
and the heart of a woolly mammoth
were blueprints in the files

He could not see beyond the skin
until he flayed it from another
and he could not see beyond the blood
until it splashed and stained his shoes
He could not see into the bone
until he cracked and split it open
But all he saw were empty chambers
dark
even under fluorescent lights
He could not see beyond the bone
which built the blood that carried love
into fingertips and dreams
He could not see beyond the bone

My love is strung with the ancient

How do I love thee   thou inward old
son of a bitch   thou self-dried
self-jailed walking gray wall of prison
guntowers & rusted barbwire   thou

inadvertent passer of genes who
gave me this face this one short leg   this
cowboy walk?   didst the half of me burn as
it passed through thy cock?   didst thou

weaken in the knees?   did the thread of
blood between us vibrate with
these days when I walk by thee   past thee
through thee as if I don't know how

thee hates thine own face   as if
I don't know how an electric razor lets
thee shave by feel & I must ask: Is it true
vampires cannot manipulate mirrors?

I love thee with the rage of the setting
sun in my bones   in the marrow of them   in
their latticed design   in my larynx   in
the timbre of my

hello to everyone but thee   (these
I acknowledge   love thee   but this body
was one of nine accidents)   I love
thee with all the scars of acne   the blackheads —

submerged poison in my flesh   I love thee with
the rage of the setting sun   with
the temperature of cigarette coals   My
love is strung with the ancient

sinews of tyrannosaurs   their extravagantly
muscled hips & perpetual coil-spring
hind-legs   their heads of mostly jaws &
teeth   I love you with all

the destruction of hydrogen bombs   the
crushing of metal against guardrails   the
ice that creeps into cells & ruptures as
it thaws

Where I First Saw the Light

Yes, indeedy, & the fists slammin the pulpit ... I remember
Sunday nights goin ta Meetin — capital EM
I didn't think it capital, though

No sir, I'da jist as soon stead home
an played with Hot Wheels
Stead home an drove those cars
on highways built inta carpet patterns —
or done my homework, even

Anythin but hear
bout the danger my soul was in
an how Jesus Harold Christ died
on The Cross ta save
me

Anythin but suffer
the decibels, the town-crier projection of go-preachers
an see the spit flying around "soul!", "salvation!"
an all the other sacred esses

Anythin but see,
behind a shout-reddened face,
the map of the Straight an Narrow Path I wasn't on
an the Broad Road ta Hell I was treadin
(water!)
because I hadn't thrown my heart's door widely open …

Yah, I bin ta hell an I think twice b'fore sayin,
"Safe as a church."

In Lieu of Flowers

for John A. (Jack) MacKenzie

So long, Jack. I didn't know ya well,
tho I am yer namesake, or woulda bin ...
But yer salesman brother, the discounter, hacked the Jack off me
b'fore it could fairly root itself in —
As you will root, I hope, down through yer coffin;
of wood, I hope,

so ya kin burst it apart as ya sprout that brush-cut up through earth
ta be trimmed back near as close by the groundskeeper's mower;
so ya kin sprout out an out b'yond the civilized fenced-in dead
ta sway with wind in fields,
ta dance with timothy an clover,
ta be the tangled silk around ears o' corn some MacPherson or Dunville
believes he planted,
ta lie matted here an there, braided with the scent of coyotes . . .

So long, Jack Giantkiller, Jack an the Beanstalk,
so long, sly Jack with seven-league boots an a belt proclaimin "Seven
with one blow!"
Yer Jack in the Box, now. B'yond flies . . . (an yer neighbours are makin,
"Ah well's ... so, then's ... sorry ta hear about ..."
an all the others, those strangely shaped sounds that never quite fit the
hole).

So long, Jack the carpenter, Jack o' All Trades
(ya did a bit o' ev'rything, I'm told).
Aw, ya'll alw'ys be Jack Carpenter ta me,
seein' as yer mother lived her last days o' strong, sweet tea in a house
that you built.

I know I saw wood when I saw you, Jack;
yer skin had the colour an' grain o' aged ash.
I saw ya solid, heavy an' lastin as bird's-eye maple
in the back room.

So long, Jack. An never mind that a mahogany-dark tale
lingers among neighbours —
a tale o' the Western Road near the Bloomfield Corner,
o' metal an' flesh an the imprint o' someone-or-another's grill on a chest,
an blood on a bumper.
But not yer bumper. Case dismissed.

An' six? seven?
years later a woman home from Kay-beck tells yer schoolteachin brother
o' lookin northwest,
past bug specks an blood, at a dark New Bruns'ick highway.

Ah well, Jack. I've driven that Western Road with bottle after bottle
warmin b'tween me thighs.
An, from the O'Leary Road one June,
I saw the sculpture o' you mowin grass.
I stopped, but our tongues were wood,
the lawnmower muttered,
an the Plymouth's Slant Six ticked towards July, ticked
towards bein upside-down in a litter of glass b'side the road
while I furrowed the clay shoulder with mine —

An the hitchhiker?
Well sir, she crawled out b'tween crumpled roof an door,
kept hikin.
I know we both coulda bin in coffins, or b'tween spoked wheels.
Ah, well.

So long, Jack. Maybe I'll gain some weight,
or cut me hair an watch coyotes lounge at twilight
under an orange moon.

Mouths Hunger

somewhere in the middle of this Island
god spoke blood, the soil drank

in brooks, the trout learned sacrifice
became priests of the food chain

lupins howled colourful praise
death was mother to all
against the duty of life

the sun did not come up
the moon was weary, pale lies
fell into mouths, hungry

the wildflowers begged for water dishes
humour was a thirst

the soil drank god

The Integrity of Life and Death

So life and death stand in a ditch
flowers and wild oats tearing at their knees

and life tells death that all this is hers
and he is a trespasser.

She says: death, you're a gun
in the hand of a stranger
and never the smile on the face of kin.

Death is hungry, and says to life
that the stars are teeth —
galaxies eat the sky ... and anyway, he says

guns are beautiful —
all metal, machined by artists
who have found a way to be paid

and also, guns are flowers —
bullets their flown seeds.

Without me, says death,
there'd be no room for you, life,
on battlefields rainbowed with petals, and deafening
with the devouring hum of bees and wasps.

And listen … if you had any kin
they'd be stitched to gallows
under a blind and turning silver eye.

Life has no answer but her stranglehold.
And so there they stand, thighs all wrapped
in mustard and browning timothy. And death laughing

The Farmer Thinks About Cows and Fish

"Hard birth this morning," he says. "Breech."
And stands looking at the Strait.
"Had to reach in and turn it in the canal. Still wouldn't come;
Like it didn't want to be born, y'know …

"Then had to rig a halter on the cow,
Hitch her to the pen so I could get at it with the chain pullers.
Hate using them pullers — don't seem right,
Metal being so close to a womb; metal so near to being
The first thing felt in this world …

"But what're ya gonna do? Gotta use 'em, or
The birth canal might's well be a spiked gun barrel …
Only worse, 'cause ya can always *not* use a gun, but
Living tissue? It's locked into musts,
It does or dies.

"So I wrapped the pullers behind those wet hooves
And leaned back, pulling steady like ya gotta do —
Keeping the pressure constant so's not to tear her
Or the calf. And all the time her head swivelling
On the line hitched to the pen like she was spitted on it;
And lowing a long, b-flat bawl that ya could believe was
The horn in the lighthouse at the Point.

"Till her hind legs went all spraddled
As her hips sunk and swayed, and the calf come all at once,
Looking like some misbegotten fish
They say ya might find in the Great Lakes these days,
Flopping down all wet and shiny in the straw*...
Yuh. Hard birth. Seems like every calf there ever was
Had joined its birth's reluctance to that one.

"I got down by its head and cleared its nostrils.
And she stood there with her head down,
Trying to suck in all the air in the world,
Flanks heaving and shuddering till
Ya'd think her ribs were gonna break from her breathing,
Pushing the afterbirth out ...Well, better git at that seed drill, I s'pose —
Be on the land soon, if this weather holds."

He lifts his cap and resettles it, turns his eyes from the Strait.
"Glad I'm not a fisherman —
sure, I've got my griefs with god and the government;
But at least I know when my stock is breeding,
And I get to plant what I hope to harvest."

The Whole Shebang

yer blood is full a hammers
flashin cold in Autumn sunlight
swung by miles-long gangs twistin
veins aroun bends in limbs

yer blood is not yer own
all that rattle & bang, ring & clang
the whole shebang belongs ta an expansionist god
a manifest destiny deity
moonlightin as a construction engineer —
yer blood is his way inta yer brain

yer blood's full a the bang bang bang
that speaks a arterial walls spiked alongside tendons &
the higher tang ting a capillaries fastened
with muscle-wrenchin overhead swings
ta the underside a skin

& that poundin in yer temples is
preparation fer dynamite, shaped charges ta extend
the right-a-way through yer skull

yer blood's full a hammers layin track
fer freight trains
fer miles & miles a boxcars jammed with love
tankers brimmed with satisfaction
flatcars piled with lengths a longin —
the entire gross national product a yer mind clackin south

& ya can't sit still, can ya?
all that noise & vibration leakin through ya, drives ya
inta more production, strips ya bare

leaves the landscape a yer mind ripped & torn
yer eyes dulled & starin up past
the cluckin faces somberin dutifully
at yer wake

Momentary Silver
(Between Sackville & the Sea)

on the dike between Sackville & the sea
the marshes wet & salty where
Sir Charles Goddam Roberts sat in union with Earth
his pen licking tree limbs & marsh grasses   his
body one throb repeated & repeated still

here in the night under Orion, the Pleiades tiny
rising shyly & watching & Ursa Major
the Great Bear snuffling grunting through me   His
clumsy delicate paws my sudden force on your nipples &

all these crickets quickening tones
dopplering sound towards shrill & the Bear
            rough-furred   damp as the marshes
            all slope-shouldered muscle of want
            rolling His peculiar gait into
            a moment compressed & silvery-skittish as mercury
groans a long guttural half-howl as I grasp
transience in the lines of my palms &

we are momentary silver   each bristled follicle of
us gleaming beyond electroplated white & extruding
wire
strands that slide whole through us & on   but

the sky pulls Him back, splashing
into cooling pools swirling with surface impurities &
we shift slowly (but the Big Dipper tilts,
one drop of silver poised on its brim

the machinery of my tongue, this scent of a flower

the machinery of my tongue has seized
its pulleys pulled aslant into tangles of cables
and the camshaft snapped, half of it pushed back
into a mystifying conglomeration of cogs
now broken from their pins
and sent pinging
against the backs of my teeth

the machinery of my tongue has seized
because I found this scent of a flower
blown,
the cold wind biting notches out of perfume

I cupped it in my hands, this scent,
and it became silky, grew
the blurred wings of hummingbirds, hovered
against my lip, dove through nostrils and slammed
a sudden monkey-wrench in the gears of my throat

O We Burnt Out Our Clutches
(Riding Them Buggies of Need)

I pursued you until you became
The pursuer;
Ran me down bright streets blossomed with prostitutes of the word

Between the bones of factories
Where all the jammed and cross-purposed machinery of love rusted.
Thought was a switch frozen between the grotesque and the sacred,
Between gap and closure.

(Now this mouth has bid farewell to words —
These eyes have seen too many vowels spread into stained, white wings.
And there remains no way to tell you.)

O we clutched our secrets as we clutched one another
Till we slipped through each other's clutches —
O we burnt out our clutches.
And we shattered the gears of our love.

The Idea of Beauty (Spoke Itself)

I have been waiting here for you since
the stars first leapt into the sky
since before there was water sprung from fresh rock
(its first & longest music a metronome —
beat after unvaried beat falling like hammers of zombied blacksmiths)

I have been waiting here where
there were no flowers & the rocks were sharp
the soil odorless & dense,
no air pockets, no tunnels of worms winding
under roots of grass

I have waited here as minerals & salts turned to algae & coral
in the factory din of water & wind
as the assembly-line sun flung super-cooled windsurfing dimetrodons
among giant treeferns & monochrome blossoms,
as prototype blood shifted towards red & DNA began its fall
from beautiful flux into fixity & self-replication

I have waited here glacially for you
as the whispery respiration of trees built air
while whole forests fell into peat bogs, became stones
while the beaded sweat of ancient lives accreted into diamonds
& the idea of beauty spoke itself in the lush green syllables of your eyes

tanka

Last month — March. At home,
The wild geese were black arrows.
They pierced your blue eye.
Far, far west of you, I heard
Their dark song echo in waves.

About the Author

John MacKenzie was born on Prince Edward Island in 1968, "one of nine children of a former schoolteacher, and a reformed-alcoholic ex-sailor turned vacuum-cleaner salesman and tent preacher." He quit school in grade seven. At thirteen, he was in reform school. At nineteen, he began to write poetry and travel across Canada. He has worked in sawmills, bakeries and kitchens, and on farms and construction crews. He lives in Charlottetown, PEI, where he is on the editorial board of *blue SHIFT: A Journal of Poetry*.

CHRISTINE TRAINOR

Polestar takes pride in creating books that enrich our understanding of the world, and in introducing superb writers to discriminating readers. These voices illuminate our history, stretch the imagination and engage our sympathies.

POETRY:

Beatrice Chancy • *by George Elliott Clarke*

Shortlisted for the Atlantic Poetry Prize and the Dartmouth Book Prize. This brilliant dramatic poem is the first literary work to treat the issue of Canadian slavery. "Clarke ... carries this story from our heads to our hearts to that gut feeling we all get when we have heard a devastating truth." — NIKKI GIOVANNI

1-896095-94-1 • $16.95 CAN/$14.95 USA

Whylah Falls: Tenth Anniversary Edition • *by George Elliott Clarke*

This beautiful edition of a Canadian classic features a section of previously unpublished poems and a fascinating introduction about the writing of the poems. "*Whylah Falls* might be — dare I say it? — a great book ... I, for one, am humbled by it, am grateful for it." — PHIL HALL in *Books in Canada*

1-896095-50-X PB; 1-896095-52-6 CLOTH • $18.95 CAN/$15.95 USA PB; $24.94 CAN/$21.95 USA

I Knew Two Metis Women • *by Gregory Scofield*

Stunning in their range and honesty, these poems about Scofield's mother and aunt are a rich, multi-voice tribute to a generation of First Nations people.

0-896095-96-8 • $16.95 CAN/$14.95 USA

Inward to the Bones • *by Kate Braid*

Winner of the VanCity Book Prize. In 1930, Emily Carr met Georgia O'Keeffe at an exhibition in New York. Inspired by this meeting, poet Kate Braid describes what might have happened afterwards.

1-896095-40-2 • $16.95 CAN/$13.95 USA

FICTION:

diss/ed banded nation • *by David Nandi Odhiambo*

"Thoroughly convincing in its evocation of young, rebellious, impoverished urban lives ... an immersion into a simmering stew of racial and cultural identities..." — *The Globe and Mail*

1-896095-26-7 • $16.95 CAN/$13.95 USA

Pool-Hopping and Other Stories • *by Anne Fleming*

Shortlisted for the Governor-General's Award, the Ethel Wilson Fiction Prize and the Danuta Gleed Award. "Fleming's evenhanded, sharp-eyed and often hilarious narratives traverse the frenzied chaos of urban life with ease and precision." — *The Georgia Straight*

1-896095-18-6 • $16.95 CAN/$13.95 USA